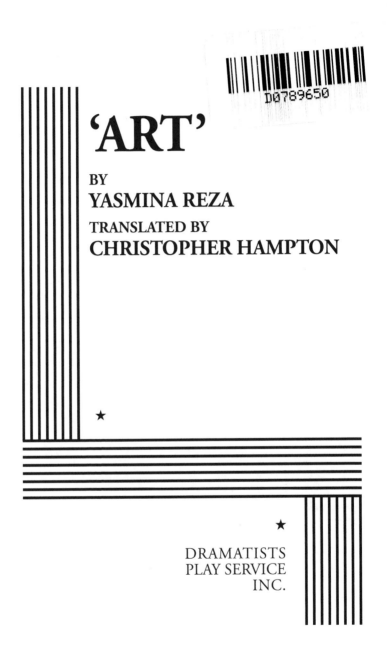

'ART'

BY
YASMINA REZA

TRANSLATED BY
CHRISTOPHER HAMPTON

★

**DRAMATISTS
PLAY SERVICE
INC.**

'ART'
Copyright © 1996, Yasmina Reza (author)
and Christopher Hampton (translator)

All Rights Reserved

SPECIAL NOTE

'ART'
by Yasmina Reza
translated by Christopher Hampton

'ART' was produced on Broadway by David Pugh, Sean Connery and Joan Cullman, at the Royale Theatre, on March 1, 1998. The associate producers were Dafydd Rogers and Stuart Thompson. It was directed by Matthew Warchus; the set design was by Mark Thompson; the lighting design was by Hugh Vanstone; the music was composed by Gary Yershon; the sound design was by Mic Pool; and the production stage manager was William Joseph Barnes. The cast was as follows:

MARC	Alan Alda
SERGE	Victor Garber
YVAN	Alfred Molina

'ART' was produced by David Pugh and Sean Connery at Wyndhams Theatre, in London, England, on October 15, 1996. It was directed by Matthew Warchus; the set design was by Mark Thompson; the lighting design was by Hugh Vanstone; and the music was composed by Gary Yershon. The cast was as follows:

MARC	Albert Finney
SERGE	Tom Courtenay
YVAN	Ken Stott

CHARACTERS

MARC
SERGE
YVAN

SETTING

The main room of an apartment.

A single set. As stripped down and neutral as possible.

The scenes unfold, successively, at Serge's, Yvan's and Marc's.

Nothing changes, except for the painting on the wall.

'ART'

MARC.   My friend Serge has bought a painting. It's a canvas about five feet by four: white. The background is white and if you screw up your eyes, you can make out some fine white diagonal lines.

Serge is one of my oldest friends.

He's done very well for himself, he's a dermatologist and he's really into *art*.

On Monday, I went over to see the painting; Serge had actually got hold of it on Saturday, but he'd been lusting after it for several months.

This white painting with white lines.

* * *

(At Serge's. At floor level, a white canvas with fine white diagonal streaks. Serge looks at his painting, thrilled. Marc looks at the painting. Serge looks at Marc looking at the painting. Long silence: from both of them, a whole range of wordless emotions.)

MARC.   Expensive?
SERGE.   Two hundred thousand.
MARC.   Two hundred thousand?
SERGE.   Jean Delauney would take it off my hands for two hundred and twenty.
MARC.   Who's that?
SERGE.   Delauney?
MARC.   Never heard of him.
SERGE.   Jean Delauney! The Delauney gallery!
MARC.   The Delauney gallery would take it off your hands for two twenty?

SERGE. No, not the gallery. Him. Delauney himself. For his own collection.

MARC. So why didn't Delauney buy it?

SERGE. It's important for them to sell to private clients. That's how the market circulates.

MARC. Uh huh ...

SERGE. Well? *(Marc says nothing.)*

You're not in the right place. Look at it from this angle. Can you see the lines?

MARC. What's the name of the ... ?

SERGE. Painter. Antrios.

MARC. Well known?

SERGE. Very. Very! *(Pause.)*

MARC. Serge, you haven't bought this painting for two hundred thousand francs?

SERGE. You don't understand, that's what it costs. It's an Antrios.

MARC. You haven't bought this painting for two hundred thousand francs?

SERGE. I might have known you'd miss the point.

MARC. You paid two hundred thousand francs for this shit?

* * *

SERGE. *(As if alone.)* My friend Marc's an intelligent enough guy. I've always valued our relationship, he has a good job, he's an aeronautical engineer, but he's one of those new-style intellectuals, who are not only enemies of modernism, but seem to take some sort of incomprehensible pride in running it down ...

In recent years these nostalgia-merchants have become quite breathtakingly arrogant.

* * *

(Same pair. Same painting. Same place. Pause.)

SERGE. What do you mean, "this shit"?

6

MARC.   Serge, where's your sense of humor? Why aren't you laughing? ... It's fantastic, you buying this painting. *(Marc laughs. Serge remains stony.)*

SERGE.   I don't care how fantastic you think it is, I don't mind if you laugh, but I would like to know what you mean by "this shit."

MARC.   You're kidding!

SERGE.   No, I'm not. By whose standards is it shit? If you call something shit, you need to have some criterion to judge it by.

MARC.   Who are you talking to? Who do you think you're talking to? Hello!

SERGE.   You have no interest whatsoever in contemporary painting, you never have. This is a field about which you know absolutely nothing, so how can you assert that any given object, which conforms to laws you don't understand, is shit?

MARC.   Because it is. It's shit. I'm sorry.

* * *

SERGE.   *(Alone.)* He doesn't like the painting.
Fine ...
But there was no warmth in the way he reacted.
No attempt.
No warmth when he dismissed it without a thought.
Just that vile pretentious laugh.
A real know it all laugh.
I hated that laugh.

* * *

MARC.   *(Alone.)* It's a complete mystery to me, Serge buying this painting. It's unsettled me, it's filled me with some indefinable unease. When I left his place, I had to take three pellets of Gelsemium 9C which Paula recommended — Gelsemium or Ignatia, she said, Gelsemium or Ignatia, which do you prefer, I mean, how the hell should I know? — because I couldn't begin to understand how Serge, my friend, could have bought that picture.

Two hundred thousand francs!

He's comfortable, but he's not rolling in money.

Comfortable, that's all, just comfortable. And he spends two hundred grand on a white painting.

I have to go see Yvan, he's a friend of ours, I have to discuss this with Yvan. Although Yvan's a very tolerant guy, which of course, when it comes to relationships, is the worst thing you can be. Yvan's tolerant because he couldn't care less.

If Yvan tolerates the fact that Serge has spent two hundred grand on some piece of white shit, it means he couldn't care less about Serge. Obviously.

* * *

(At Yvan's. On the wall, some motel painting. Yvan is on all fours with his back to us. He seems to be looking for something underneath a piece of furniture. As he does so, he turns to introduce himself.)

YVAN. I'm Yvan.

I'm a little tense at the moment, because, having spent my life in textiles, I've just found a new job as a sales agent for a wholesale stationery business.

People like me. My professional life has always been a failure and I'm getting married in two weeks. She's a lovely intelligent girl from a good family. *(Marc enters. Yvan has resumed his search and has his back to him.)*

MARC. What are you doing?

YVAN. I'm looking for the top to my pen. *(Time passes.)*

MARC. All right, that's enough.

YVAN. I had it five minutes ago.

MARC. It doesn't matter.

YVAN. Yes, it does. *(Marc gets down on his knees to help him look. Both of them spend some time looking. Marc straightens up.)*

MARC. Forget about it. Buy another one.

YVAN. It's a very special felt tip. It writes on any surface ... It's infuriating. Objects, I can't tell you how much they infuriate me. I had it in my hand five minutes ago.

MARC. Are you going to live here?

YVAN. Do you think it's suitable for a young couple?

MARC. Young couple! Ha, ha ...

YVAN. Try not to laugh like that in front of Catherine.

MARC. How's the stationery business?

YVAN. All right. I'm learning.

MARC. You've lost weight.

YVAN. A little. I'm pissed off about that top. It'll all dry up. Sit down.

MARC. If you keep on looking for that top, I'm leaving.

YVAN. Okay, I'll stop. You want something to drink?

MARC. A Perrier, if you have one. Have you seen Serge lately?

YVAN. No. Have you?

MARC. Yesterday.

YVAN. Is he okay?

MARC. Yes. He just bought a painting.

YVAN. Oh yes?

MARC. Yes.

YVAN. Nice?

MARC. White.

YVAN. White?

MARC. White. Imagine a canvas about five feet by four ... with a white background ... completely white in fact ... with fine white diagonal stripes ... you know ... and maybe another horizontal white line, toward the bottom ...

YVAN. How can you see them?

MARC. What?

YVAN. These white lines. If the background's white, how can you see the lines?

MARC. You just can. Because I suppose the lines are slightly grey, or vice versa, or anyway there are degrees of white! There's more than one kind of white!

YVAN. Don't get upset. Why are you getting upset?

MARC. You immediately start quibbling. Why can't you let me finish?

YVAN. All right. Go on.

MARC. Right. So, you have an idea of what the painting looks like.

YVAN. I think so, yes.

MARC. Now you have to guess how much Serge paid for it.

YVAN. Who's the painter?

MARC. Antrios. Ever heard of him?

YVAN. No. Is he fashionable?

MARC. I knew you were going to ask me that!

YVAN. Well, it's logical ...

MARC. No, it's not logical ...

YVAN. Of course it's logical, you ask me to guess the price, you know very well the price depends on how fashionable the painter is ...

MARC. I'm not asking you to apply a whole set of critical standards, I'm not asking you for a professional estimate, I'm asking you what you, Yvan, would pay for a white painting gussied up with a few off-white stripes.

YVAN. Jack shit.

MARC. Right. And what about Serge? Pick a figure at random.

YVAN. Ten thousand francs.

MARC. Ha!

YVAN. Fifty thousand.

MARC. Ha!

YVAN. A hundred thousand.

MARC. Keep going.

YVAN. A hundred and fifty? Two hundred?!

MARC. Two hundred. Two hundred grand.

YVAN. No!

MARC. Yes.

YVAN. Two hundred grand?

MARC. Two hundred grand.

YVAN. Has he gone crazy?

MARC. Looks like it. *(Slight pause.)*

YVAN. All the same ...

MARC. What do you mean, all the same?

YVAN. If it makes him happy ... he can afford it ...

MARC. So that's what you think, huh?

YVAN. Why? What do you think?

MARC. You don't understand the seriousness of this, do you?

YVAN. Er ... no.

MARC. It's strange how you're missing the basic point of this story. All you can see is externals. You don't understand the seriousness of it.

YVAN.   What is the seriousness of it?

MARC.   You don't understand what this means?

YVAN.   You want a cashew?

MARC.   You don't see that suddenly, in some grotesque way, Serge sees himself as a "collector."

YVAN.   Well ...

MARC.   From now on, our friend Serge is one of the great connoisseurs.

YVAN.   Bullshit.

MARC.   Of course it's bullshit. You can't buy your way in that cheap. But that's what he thinks.

YVAN.   Oh, I see.

MARC.   Doesn't that bother you?

YVAN.   No. Not if it makes him happy.

MARC.   If it makes him happy. What's that supposed to mean? What kind of a philosophy is that, if it makes him happy?

YVAN.   As long as it's not doing harm to anyone else ...

MARC.   But it is, it is doing harm to me! I'm disturbed, I'm disturbed, more than that, I'm hurt, yes, I am. I'm fond of Serge and to see him let himself be ripped off and lose every ounce of discernment through sheer snobbery ...

YVAN.   I don't know why you're so surprised. He's always haunted art galleries like crazy. He's always been an exhibition freak.

MARC.   He's always been a freak, but a freak with a sense of humor. You see, basically, what really upsets me is that you can't laugh with him anymore.

YVAN.   I'm sure you can.

MARC.   You can't!

YVAN.   Have you tried?

MARC.   Of course I've tried. I laughed. Heartily. What do you think I did? He didn't crack a smile. Although, two hundred grand, that's kind of an expensive laugh.

YVAN.   Yes. *(They laugh.)* I'll make him laugh.

MARC.   I'd be amazed. Any more nuts?

YVAN.   He'll laugh, you'll see.

* * *

(At Serge's. Serge is with Yvan. The painting isn't there.)

SERGE.   ... and you get along with the in-laws?

YVAN.   Wonderfully. As far as they're concerned, I'm just some jerk stumbling from one iffy job to another and I'm now groping my way into the world of vellum ... This thing on my hand, what is it? *(Serge examines it.)* Is it serious?

SERGE.   No.

YVAN.   Oh, good. So what's new?

SERGE.   Nothing. Lot of work. Exhausted. It's nice to see you. You never call.

YVAN.   I don't like to disturb you.

SERGE.   You're kidding, you just speak to my secretary and I'll call you right back.

YVAN.   I guess so. Your place gets more and more monastic ... *(Serge laughs.)*

SERGE.   Yes! Seen Marc lately?

YVAN.   Not lately, no. Have you?

SERGE.   Two or three days ago.

YVAN.   Is he all right?

SERGE.   Yes. More or less.

YVAN.   Oh?

SERGE.   No, he's all right.

YVAN.   I talked to him on the phone last week, he seemed all right.

SERGE.   Well, he is. He's all right.

YVAN.   You seemed to be implying he wasn't all right.

SERGE.   On the contrary, I said he was all right.

YVAN.   More or less, you said.

SERGE.   Yes, more or less. More or less all right. *(Long silence. Yvan wanders around the room.)*

YVAN.   You been out? Seen anything?

SERGE.   No. I can't afford to go out.

YVAN.   Oh?

SERGE.   *(Cheerfully.)* I'm ruined.

YVAN.   Oh?

SERGE.   You want to see something special? Would you like to?

YVAN.   Sure I would. Show me. *(Serge exits and returns with the Antrios, which he turns around and sets down in front of Yvan. Yvan looks at the painting and, strangely enough, doesn't manage the hearty laugh he'd predicted. A long pause, while Yvan studies the painting and Serge studies Yvan.)* Ah, yes. Yes, yes.

SERGE.   Antrios.

YVAN.   Yes, yes.

SERGE.   It's a seventies Antrios. Worth mentioning. He's going through a similar phase now, but this one's from the seventies.

YVAN.   Yes, yes. Expensive?

SERGE.   In absolute terms, yes. In fact, no. You like it?

YVAN.   Ah, yes, yes, yes.

SERGE.   Plain.

YVAN.   Plain, yes ... Yes ... And at the same time ...

SERGE.   Magnetic.

YVAN.   Mm ... yes ...

SERGE.   You don't really get the resonance just at the moment.

YVAN.   Well, a little ...

SERGE.   No, you don't. You have to come back in the middle of the day. That resonance you get from something monochromatic, it doesn't really happen under artificial light.

YVAN.   Aha.

SERGE.   Not that it is actually monochromatic.

YVAN.   Oh, no ... How much?

SERGE.   Two hundred thousand.

YVAN.   Very reasonable.

SERGE.   Very. *(Silence. Suddenly Serge bursts out laughing, immediately followed by Yvan. Both of them roar with laughter.)* Crazy, or what?

YVAN.   Crazy!

SERGE.   Two hundred thousand. *(Hearty laughter. They stop. They look at each other. They start again. Then stop. They've calmed down.)* You know Marc's seen this painting.

YVAN.   Oh?

SERGE.   Devastated.

YVAN. Oh?

SERGE. He told me it was shit. A completely inappropriate description.

YVAN. Absolutely.

SERGE. You can't call this shit.

YVAN. No.

SERGE. You can say, I don't get it, I can't grasp it, you can't say "it's shit."

YVAN. You've seen his place.

SERGE. Nothing to see. It's like yours. It's ... What I mean is, you couldn't care less.

YVAN. His taste is classical, he likes things classical, what do you expect ...

SERGE. He started in with this sardonic laugh ... Not a trace of charm ... Not a trace of humor.

YVAN. You know Marc is moody. Nothing new about that.

SERGE. He has no sense of humor. With you, I can laugh. With him, I'm like a block of ice.

YVAN. It's true he's a little gloomy right now.

SERGE. I don't blame him for not responding to this painting, he doesn't have the training, there's a whole apprenticeship you have to go through, which he hasn't, either because he's never wanted to or because he has no particular instinct for it, none of that matters, no, what I blame him for is his tone of voice, his smugness, his tactlessness. I blame him for his insensitivity. I don't blame him for not being interested in modern art, I couldn't give a shit about that, I like him for other reasons ...

YVAN. And he likes you!

SERGE. No, no, no, no, I felt it the other day, a kind of ... a kind of condescension ... contempt with a really bitter edge ...

YVAN. No!

SERGE. Yes! Don't keep trying to smooth things over. Where d'you get this urge to be the great reconciler of the human race? Why don't you admit that Marc is atrophying? If he hasn't already atrophied. *(Silence.)*

* * *

(At Marc's. On the wall, a figurative painting: a landscape seen through a window.)

YVAN.   We laughed.

MARC.   You laughed?

YVAN.   We laughed. Both of us. We laughed. I promise you on Catherine's life, we had a good laugh, both of us, together.

MARC.   You told him it was shit and you had a good laugh.

YVAN.   No, I didn't tell him it was shit, we laughed spontaneously.

MARC.   You arrived, you looked at the painting and you laughed. And then he laughed.

YVAN.   Yes. Something like that. We talked a little and then it was pretty much the way you described it.

MARC.   And it was a genuine laugh.

YVAN.   Perfectly genuine.

MARC.   Well, then, I've made a mistake. Good. I'm really pleased to hear it.

YVAN.   It was even better than you think. It was Serge who laughed first.

MARC.   It was Serge who laughed first ...

YVAN.   Yes.

MARC.   He laughed first and you joined in.

YVAN.   Yes.

MARC.   But what made him laugh?

YVAN.   He laughed because he sensed I was about to laugh. I guess he laughed to put me at my ease.

MARC.   It doesn't count if he laughed first. If he laughed first it was to defuse your laughter. It means it wasn't a genuine laugh.

YVAN.   It was a genuine laugh.

MARC.   It might have been a genuine laugh, but it wasn't for the right reason.

YVAN.   What is the right reason? I'm confused.

MARC.   He wasn't laughing because his painting is ridiculous, you and he weren't laughing for the same reasons, you were laughing at the painting and he was laughing to ingratiate himself, to put himself on your wavelength, to show that on top of being an aesthete who can spend more on a painting than you earn in a year, he's still the same old rebellious pal you used to kid around with.

YVAN.   Mm hm ... *(A brief silence.)* You know ...

MARC.   Yes ...

YVAN.   This is going to amaze you ...

MARC.   Go on ...

YVAN.   I didn't like the painting ... but I didn't actually hate it.

MARC.   Well, of course not. You can't hate what's invisible, you can't hate nothing.

YVAN.   No, no it has something ...

MARC.   What do you mean?

YVAN.   It has something. It's not nothing.

MARC.   You're kidding.

YVAN.   I'm not as harsh as you. It's a work of art, there's a system behind it.

MARC.   A system?

YVAN.   A system.

MARC.   What system?

YVAN.   It's the completion of a journey ...

MARC.   Ha, ha, ha!

YVAN.   It wasn't painted by accident, it's a work of art which stakes its claim as part of a trajectory ...

MARC.   Ha, ha, ha!

YVAN.   Go ahead, laugh.

MARC.   You're parroting all of Serge's nonsense. From him it's heart-breaking, from you its just comical!

YVAN.   You know, Marc, this smugness, you want to watch that. You're getting bitter, it not very attractive.

MARC.   Good. The older I get, the more offensive I hope to become.

YVAN.   Great.

MARC.   A system!

YVAN.   You're impossible to talk to.

MARC.   There's a system behind it! ... You look at this piece of shit, but never mind, never mind, there's a system behind it! ...

You think there's a system behind this landscape? *(He indicates the painting on his wall.)* ... No, uh? Too evocative. Too expressive. Everything's on the canvas! No scope for a system! ...

YVAN.   I'm glad you're enjoying yourself.

MARC.   Yvan, look, speak for yourself. Describe your feelings to me.

YVAN.   I felt a resonance.

MARC.   You felt a resonance? ...

YVAN.   You're denying that I'm capable of appreciating this painting for myself.

MARC.   Of course I am.

YVAN.   Well, why?

MARC.   Because I know you. Because apart from being disastrously open-minded, you're quite sane.

YVAN.   I wish I could say the same for you.

MARC.   Yvan, look me in the eye.

YVAN.   I'm looking at you.

MARC.   Were you moved by Serge's painting?

YVAN.   No.

MARC.   Answer me this. You and Catherine get this painting as a wedding present. Does it make you happy? ... Does it make you happy? ...

*   *   *

YVAN.   *(Alone.)* Of course it doesn't make me happy.

It doesn't make me happy, but, generally speaking I'm not the sort of person who can say I'm happy, just like that.

I'm trying to ... I'm trying to think of an occasion when I could have said yes, I'm happy ... Are you happy to be getting married, my mother stupidly asked me one day, are you at least happy to be getting married? ... Why wouldn't I be?

What do you mean, why wouldn't I be? You're either happy or you're not happy, what's why wouldn't I be got to do with it? ...

*   *   *

17

SERGE.   *(Alone.)* As far as I'm concerned, it's not white.

When I say as far as I'm concerned, I mean objectively. Objectively speaking, it's not white.

It has a white background, with a whole range of greys ... There's even some red in it.

You could say it's very pale.

I wouldn't like it if it was white. Marc thinks it's white ... that's his limit ...

Marc thinks it's white because he's gotten hung up on the idea that it's white.

Unlike Yvan. Yvan can see it isn't white.

Marc can think what he likes, what do I care?

* * *

MARC.   *(Alone.)* Obviously I should have taken the Ignatia.

Why do I have to be so categorical?

What possible difference can it make to me, if Serge lets himself be taken in by modern Art?

I mean, it is a serious matter. But I could have found some other way to put it to him.

I could have used a less aggressive tone.

Even if it makes me physically ill that my best friend has bought a white painting, all the same I ought to avoid attacking him about it.

I have to be nicer to him.

From now on, I'm on my best behaviour.

* * *

(At Serge's.)

SERGE.   Feel like a laugh?
MARC.   Go on.
SERGE.   Yvan liked the Antrios.
MARC.   Where is it?

18

SERGE. You want another look?

MARC. Let me see it.

SERGE. I knew you'd come around to it. *(He exits and returns with the painting. A moment of contemplation.)* Yvan got it. Right away.

MARC. Uh huh.

SERGE. All right, listen, it's just a picture, we don't have to get bogged down with it, life's too short ... By the way, have you read this? *(He picks up* De Vita Beata *by Seneca and throws it on to the low table just in front of Marc.)* Read it, it's a masterpiece. *(Marc picks up the book, opens it and leafs through it.)* Incredibly modern. Read that, you don't need to read anything else. What with the office, the hospital, Françoise, who's now decreed that I should see the children every weekend — which is something new for Francoise, the notion that children need a father — I don't have time to read any more, I'm obliged to go straight for the essentials.

MARC. ... As in painting ... Where you've ingeniously eliminated form and color. Those old chestnuts.

SERGE. Yes ... Although I'm still capable of appreciating more figurative work.

Like your Flemish number. Very restful.

MARC. What's Flemish about it? It's a view of Carcassonne.

SERGE. Yes, but I mean ... it's slightly Flemish in style ... the window, the view, the ... in any case, it's very pretty.

MARC. It's not worth anything, you know that.

SERGE. What difference does that make? ... Anyway, in a few years God knows if the Antrios will be worth anything! ...

MARC. ... You know, I've been thinking. I've been thinking and I've changed my mind. The other day, driving across town, I was thinking about you and I said to myself: isn't there, deep down, something really poetic about what Serge has done? ... Isn't surrendering to this incoherent urge to buy in fact an authentically poetic impulse?

SERGE. You're very conciliatory today. Unrecognizable. What's this bland, submissive tone of voice? It doesn't suit you at all, by the way.

MARC. No, no, I'm trying to explain, I'm apologizing.

SERGE. Apologizing? What for?

MARC. I'm too thin-skinned, I'm too high-strung, I over-react ... You could say, I lack judgment.

SERGE. Read Seneca.

MARC. That's it. See, for instance, you say "read Seneca" and I could easily have gotten annoyed. I'm quite capable of being really annoyed by your saying to me in the course of our conversation, "read Seneca." Which is absurd of me!

SERGE. No. It's not absurd.

MARC. Really?

SERGE. No, because you thought you could identify ...

MARC. I didn't say I *was* annoyed ...

SERGE. You said you could easily ...

MARC. Yes, yes. I could easily ...

SERGE. Get annoyed, and I understand that. Because when I said "read Seneca," you thought you could identify a kind of superiority. You tell me you lack judgment and my answer is "read Seneca," well, it's obnoxious!

MARC. It is a little.

SERGE. Having said that, it's true you lack judgment, because I didn't say "read Seneca," I said "read Seneca!"

MARC. You're right. You're right.

SERGE. The fact of the matter is, you've quite simply lost your sense of humor.

MARC. Probably.

SERGE. You've lost your sense of humor, Marc. You really have lost your sense of humor. When I was talking to Yvan the other day, we agreed you'd lost your sense of humor. Where the hell is he? He's incapable of being on time, it's infuriating! We'll miss the beginning!

MARC. ... Yvan thinks I've lost my sense of humor? ...

SERGE. Yvan agrees with me that recently you've somewhat lost your sense of humor.

MARC. The last time you saw each other, Yvan said he liked your painting very much and I'd lost my sense of humor ...

SERGE. Oh yes, that, yes, the painting, really, very much. And he meant it ... What's that you're eating?

MARC.   Ignatia.

SERGE.   Oh, you believe in homeopathy now?

MARC.   I don't believe in anything.

SERGE.   Didn't you think Yvan had lost a lot of weight?

MARC.   So's she.

SERGE.   It's the wedding, eating away at them.

MARC.   Yes. *(They laugh.)*

SERGE.   How's Paula?

MARC.   All right. *(He indicates the Antrios.)* Where are you going to put it?

SERGE.   Haven't decided. There. Or there? ... Too ostentatious.

MARC.   Are you going to have it framed? *(Serge laughs discreetly.)*

SERGE.   No! ... No, no ...

MARC.   Why not?

SERGE.   It's not supposed to be framed.

MARC.   Is that right?

SERGE.   The artist doesn't want it to be. It mustn't be interrupted. It's already in its setting. *(He signals Marc over to examine the edge.)* Look ... you see ...

MARC.   What is it, adhesive tape?

SERGE.   No, it's a kind of Kraft paper ... Made up by the artist.

MARC.   It's funny the way you say the artist.

SERGE.   What else am I supposed to say?

MARC.   You say the artist when you could say the painter or ... whatever his name is ... Antrios ...

SERGE.   So?

MARC.   But you say the artist, as if he's some sort of ... well, anyway, doesn't matter. What are we seeing tonight? Let's try and see a movie with a little substance for once.

SERGE.   It's eight o'clock. Everything will have started. I can't imagine how this man, who has nothing whatsoever to do — am I right? — manages to be late every single time. Where the fuck is he?

MARC.   Let's just eat dinner.

SERGE.   All right. It's five after eight. We said we'd meet between seven and half-past ... What d'you mean, the way I say the artist?

MARC.   Nothing. I was going to say something stupid.

SERGE. Well, go on.

MARC. You say the artist as if ... as if he's some unattainable being. The artist ... some sort of god ... *(Serge laughs.)*

SERGE. Well, for me, he is a god! You don't think I'd have forked out a fortune for a mere mortal! ...

MARC. Well, no.

SERGE. I went to the Pompidou on Monday, you know how many Antrioses they have at the Pompidou? ... Three! Three Antrioses! ... At the Pompidou!

MARC. Amazing.

SERGE. And mine's as good as any of them! If not better! ... Listen, I have a suggestion, let's give Yvan exactly three more minutes and then get the hell out of here. I've found a great new place. Lyonnaise food.

MARC. Why are you so jumpy?

SERGE. I'm not jumpy.

MARC. Yes, you are jumpy.

SERGE. I am not jumpy, all right, I'm jumpy, I'm jumpy because this slackness is intolerable, this inability to practice any kind of self-discipline!

MARC. The fact is, I'm getting on your nerves and you're taking it out on poor Yvan.

SERGE. What do you mean, poor Yvan, are you shitting me? You're not getting on my nerves, why should you be getting on my nerves?

* * *

SERGE. He is getting on my nerves. It's true.

He's getting on my nerves.

It's this ingratiating tone of voice. A little smile behind every word.

It's as if he's forcing himself to be pleasant. Don't be pleasant, whatever you do, don't be pleasant!

Could it be the Antrios? ... Could buying the Antrios have triggered this feeling of constraint between us?

Buying something ... without his approval?

Well, screw his approval! Screw your approval, Marc!

* * *

22

MARC.   Could it be the Antrios, buying the Antrios?

No — It started some time ago ...

To be precise, it started on the day we were discussing some work of art and you uttered, quite seriously, the word *deconstruction*.

It wasn't so much the word deconstruction that upset me, it was the air of solemnity you imbued it with.

You said, humorlessly, unapologetically, without a trace of irony, the word deconstruction, you, my friend. I didn't know the best way to handle the situation, so I made this throwaway remark, I said I guess I must be getting intolerant in my old age, and your response was, who do you think you are? What makes you so high and mighty? ...

What gives you the right to set yourself apart? Serge responded in the shittiest possible way. And totally unexpectedly.

You're just Marc, what makes you think you're so special?

That day, I should have punched him right in the mouth. And when he was lying there on the ground, half-dead, I should have said to him, you're supposed to be my friend, what sort of a friend are you, Serge, if you don't think your friends are special?

* * *

(At Serge's. Marc and Serge, as we left them.)

MARC.   Lyonnaise, you said? Little heavy, isn't it? Little fatty, all those sausages ... what do you think? *(The doorbell rings.)*

SERGE.   Twelve minutes past eight. *(Serge goes to open the door to Yvan. Yvan walks into the room, already talking.)*

YVAN.   So, a crisis, insoluble problem, major crisis, both step-mothers want their names on the wedding invitation. Catherine adores her step-mother, who more or less brought her up, she wants her name on the invitation, she wants it and her step-mother is not anticipating, which is understandable, since the mother is dead, not appearing next to Catherine's father, whereas my step-mother, whom I detest, it's out of the question her name should appear on the invitation, but my father won't have his name on it if hers isn't, unless Catherine's step-mother is left off, which is completely unacceptable, I suggested none of the parents' names should be on it, after all we're not adolescents, we can announce our wedding and invite people ourselves, so Catherine screamed her head off, arguing that would be a slap in the face for her parents who are paying through the nose for the reception, and particularly for her step-mother, who's gone to so much trouble when she isn't even her daughter and I finally let myself be persuaded, totally against my better judgment, because she wore me down, I finally agreed that my step-mother, whom I detest, who's a complete bitch, will have her name on the invitation, so I telephone my mother to warn her, mother, I said, I've done everything I can to avoid this, but we have absolutely no choice, Colette's name has to be on the invitation, she said, if Colette's name is on the invitation, take mine off it, mother, I said, please, I beg you, don't make things even more difficult, and she said, how dare you suggest my name is left to float around the card on its own, as if I was some abandoned woman, below Colette, who'll be clamped on to your father's name, like a limpet, I said to her, mother, I have friends waiting for me, I'm going to hang up and we'll discuss all this tomorrow after a good night's sleep, she said, why is it I'm always an afterthought, what are you talking about, mother, you're not always an afterthought, of course I am and when you say don't make things even more difficult, what you mean is, everything's already been decided, everything's been organized without me, everything's been cooked up behind my back, good old Nadia, she'll agree to anything and all this, she said — get this — in aid of an event, the importance of which I'm having some trouble grasping, mother, I have friends waiting for me, that's right, there's always something better to do, anything's more important then I am, goodbye and she hung up, Catherine, who was next to me, but who hadn't heard her side of the conversation, said, what did she say, I said she doesn't want her name on the invitation with Colette, which is understandable, I'm not talking about that, what did she say about the wedding, nothing, you're lying, I'm not, Cathy, I promise you, she just doesn't want her name on the invitation with Colette, call her back and tell her when your son's getting married, you rise above your vanity, you could say the same thing to your step-mother, that's got nothing to do with it, Catherine shouted, it's me, I'm the one who's insisting her name's on it, it's not her, the poor thing, she's tact personified, if she had any idea of the problem this is causing, she'd be down on her knees, begging for her name to be taken off the invitation, now call your mother, so I called her again, by now I'm in shreds, Catherine's listening on the extension, Yvan, my mother says, up to now you've conducted your affairs in the most chaotic way imaginable and just because, out of the blue, you've decided to embark on matrimony, I find myself obliged to spend all afternoon and evening with your father, a man I haven't seen for seventeen years and to whom I was not expecting to have to reveal my hip-size and my puffy cheeks, not to mention Colette who incidentally, I may tell you, according to Felix Perolari, has now taken up bridge — my mother always played bridge — I can see all that can't be helped, but on the invitation, the one item everyone is going to receive and examine, I insist on making a solo appearance, Catherine, listening on the extension, shakes her head and screws up her face in disgust, mother, I say, why are you so selfish, I'm not selfish, I'm not selfish, Yvan, you're not going to start too, you're not going to be like Mme Romero this morning and tell me I have a heart of stone, that everybody in our family has a heart of stone, that's what Mme Romero said this morning — she's gone completely insane by the way — when I refused to raise her pay to sixty francs an hour cash, she had the gall to say everyone in the family had a heart of stone, when she knows perfectly well about poor Andre's pacemaker, you haven't even bothered to drop him a line, yes, that's right, very funny, everything's a joke to you, it's not me who's the selfish one, Yvan, you've still got a lot to learn about life, but you go, darling, go ahead, go ahead, go and see your precious friends ... *(Silence.)*

SERGE.   Then what? ...

YVAN.   Then nothing. Nothing's been resolved. I hung up. Minidrama with Catherine. Cut short, because I was late.

MARC.   Why do you let yourself be fucked over by all these women?

YVAN. Why do I let myself be fucked over, I don't know! They're all insane.

SERGE. You've lost weight.

YVAN. Of course I have. Ten pounds. Purely through stress.

MARC. Read Seneca ...

YVAN. "The Happy Life," just what I need! What's he suggest?

MARC. It's a masterpiece.

YVAN. Oh?

SERGE. He hasn't read it.

YVAN. Oh.

MARC. No, but Serge just told me it was a masterpiece.

SERGE. I said it was a masterpiece because it is a masterpiece.

MARC. Right.

SERGE. It is a masterpiece.

MARC. Why are you getting annoyed?

SERGE. You seem to be insinuating I use the word masterpiece any chance I get.

MARC. Not at all ...

SERGE. You said the word in a kind of sarcastic way ...

MARC. Not at all!

SERGE. Yes, yes the word masterpiece in a kind of ...

MARC. Is he crazy? Not at all! ... However, when you used the word, you qualified it by saying "incredibly modern."

SERGE. Yes. So?

MARC. You said "incredibly modern," as if modern was the highest compliment you could give. As if, when describing something, you couldn't think of anything more admirable, more profoundly admirable than modern.

SERGE. So?

MARC. So nothing. And please note I made no mention of the word incredibly ... Incredibly modern!

SERGE. You're really needling me today.

MARC. No, I'm not ...

YVAN. You're not going to fight, that would just about finish me off!

SERGE. You don't think it's extraordinary that a man who wrote nearly two thousand years ago should still be so completely up to date?

MARC.   No. Of course not. That's the definition of a classic.

SERGE.   You're just playing with words.

YVAN.   So, what are we going to do? I guess we can forget about the movies, I'm sorry. You want to go eat?

MARC.   Serge tells me you're very taken with his painting.

YVAN.   Yes ... I am kind of ... taken with it, yes ... You're not, I gather.

MARC.   No. Let's go eat. Serge has a very tempting recommendation. Lyonnaise.

SERGE.   You think the food's too fatty.

MARC.   I think the food's a little bit on the fatty side, but I'm willing to give it a shot.

SERGE.   No, if you think the food's too fatty, we'll find somewhere else.

MARC.   No, let's give it a shot.

SERGE.   We'll go to the restaurant if you think you'll like it. If not, we won't.

(To Yvan.) You like Lyonnaise food?

YVAN.   I'll do whatever you like.

MARC.   He'll do whatever you like. Whatever you like, he'll always do.

YVAN.   What's the matter with you? You're both acting very strange.

SERGE.   He's right, once in a while you could have an opinion of your own.

YVAN.   Listen, if you think you're going to use me as your punching bag, I'm out of here! I've put up with enough today.

MARC.   Where's your sense of humor, Yvan?

YVAN.   What?

MARC.   Where's your sense of humor, kiddo?

YVAN.   Where's my sense of humor? I don't see anything to laugh at. Where's my sense of humor, are you trying to be funny?

MARC.   I think recently you've somewhat lost your sense of humor. You better watch that, believe me!

YVAN.   What's the matter with you?

MARC.   Don't you think recently I've also somewhat lost my sense of humor?

YVAN. Oh, I see!

SERGE. All right, that's enough, let's make a decision. Tell you the truth, I'm not even hungry.

YVAN. You're both really sinister this evening.

SERGE. You want my opinion about your women problems?

YVAN. Go on.

SERGE. In my view, the most hysterical of them all is Catherine. By far.

MARC. No question.

SERGE. And if you're already letting yourself be fucked over by her, you're in for a hideous future.

YVAN. What can I do?

MARC. Cancel it.

YVAN. Cancel the wedding?

SERGE. He's right.

YVAN. But I can't, are you crazy?

MARC. Why not?

YVAN. Well, because I can't, that's all! It's all arranged. I've only been working in the stationery business for a month ...

MARC. What's that got to do with it?

YVAN. It's her uncle's stationery business, he had absolutely no need to take on anyone, least of all someone who's only ever worked in textiles.

SERGE. Do whatever you want. I've told you what I think.

YVAN. I'm sorry, Serge, I don't mean to be rude, but you're not necessarily the person I'd come to for matrimonial advice. You can't claim to have been a great success in that field ...

SERGE. Precisely.

YVAN. I can't back out of the wedding. I know Catherine is hysterical but she has her good points. There are certain crucial qualities you need when you're marrying someone like me ... *(He indicates the Antrios.)* Where are you going to put it?

SERGE. I don't know yet.

YVAN. Why don't you put it there?

SERGE. Because there, it'd be wiped out by the sunlight.

YVAN. Oh, yes. I thought of you today at the store, we ran off five hundred posters by this guy who paints white flowers, totally white, on a white background.

SERGE. The Antrios is not white.

YVAN. No, of course not. I was just saying.

MARC. You think this painting is not white, Yvan?

YVAN. Not entirely, no ...

MARC. Ah. Then what color is it?

YVAN. Various colors ... There's yellow, there's grey, some slightly ochrish lines.

MARC. And you're moved by these colors?

YVAN. Yes ... I'm moved by these colors.

MARC. You're spineless, Yvan. You have no substance, you're an amoeba.

SERGE. Why are you attacking Yvan like this?

MARC. Because he's a little ass-kisser, he's obsequious, dazzled by money, dazzled by what he believes to be culture, and as you know culture is something I absolutely piss on. *(Brief silence.)*

SERGE. ... What's gotten into you?

MARC. *(To Yvan.)* How could you, Yvan? ... And in front of me. In front of me, Yvan.

YVAN. What d'you mean, in front of you? ... What d'you mean, in front of you?

I find these colors touching. Yes. If it's all the same to you.

Stop wanting to control everything.

MARC. How could you say, in front of me, that you find these colors touching?

YVAN. Because it's the truth.

MARC. The truth? You find these colors touching?

YVAN. Yes, I find these colors touching.

MARC. You find these colors touching, Yvan!?

SERGE. He finds these colors touching! He's perfectly entitled to!

MARC. No, he's not entitled to.

SERGE. What do you mean, he's not entitled to?

MARC. He's not entitled to.

YVAN. I'm not entitled to? ...

MARC. No.

SERGE. Why is he not entitled to? I don't think you're very well. Maybe you should go and see somebody.

29

MARC. He's not entitled to say he finds these colors touching, because he doesn't.

YVAN. I don't find these colors touching?

MARC. There are no colors. You can't see them. And you don't find them touching.

YVAN. Speak for yourself!

MARC. This is really demeaning, Yvan! ...

SERGE. Who do you think you are, Marc? ...

Who are you to legislate? You don't like anything, you despise everyone. You take pride in not being a man of your time ...

MARC. What's that supposed to mean, a man of my time?

YVAN. Okay. I'm leaving.

SERGE. Where are you going?

YVAN. I'm leaving. I don't see why I have to put up with your tantrums.

SERGE. Don't go! You're not going to start taking offence, are you? ... If you go, you're giving in to him. *(Yvan stands there, hesitating, caught between two possibilities.)* A man of his time is a man who lives in his own time.

MARC. Bullshit. How can a man live in any other time but his own? Answer me that.

SERGE. A man of his time is someone of whom it can be said in twenty years or in a hundred years time, he was representative of his era.

MARC. Hm.

To what end?

SERGE. What do you mean, to what end?

MARC. What use is it to me if someday somebody says, I was representative of my era?

SERGE. Listen, sweetheart, we're not talking about you, if you can imagine such a thing! We don't give a fuck about you!

A man of his time, I'm trying to explain to you, like most people you admire, is someone who makes some kind of contribution to the human race ... A man of his time doesn't assume the history of art has come to an end with a pseudo Flemish view of Cavaillon ...

MARC. Carcassonne.

SERGE. Same thing. A man of his time plays his part in the

fundamental dynamic of evolution ...

MARC. And that's a good thing in your view?

SERGE. It's not good or bad, why do you always have to moralize, it's just the way things are.

MARC. And you, for example, you play your part in the fundamental dynamic of evolution.

SERGE. I do.

MARC. What about Yvan? ...

YVAN. Surely not. What part can an amoeba play?

SERGE. In his way, Yvan is a man of his time.

MARC. How can you tell? Not from that motel painting he has hanging on his wall!

YVAN. That is not a motel painting!

SERGE. It is a motel painting.

YVAN. It is not!

SERGE. What's the difference? Yvan represents a certain way of life, a way of thinking which is completely modern. And so do you. I'm sorry, but you're a typical man of your time. And, in fact, the harder you try not to be, the more you are.

MARC. Well, okay. Fine. So what's the problem?

SERGE. There is no problem, except for you, because you take pride in your desire to shut yourself off from humanity. And you'll never manage to. It's like you're in quicksand, the more you struggle to get out of it, the deeper you sink. Now apologize to Yvan.

MARC. Yvan is a coward. *(At this point, Yvan makes his decision: and exits in a rush. Slight pause.)*

SERGE. Bravo. *(Silence.)*

MARC. It wasn't a good idea to see each other tonight ... was it? ... I ought to go, too ...

SERGE. Maybe ...

MARC. Right.

SERGE. You're the coward ... attacking someone who's incapable of defending himself ... as you well know.

MARC. You're right ... you're right and when you put it like that, it makes me feel even worse ... the thing is, all of a sudden, I can't understand, I have no idea what binds me to Yvan ... I have no idea what my relationship with him consists of.

SERGE.   Yvan's always been what he is.

MARC.   No. He used to be eccentric, kind of absurd ... he was always unstable, but his eccentricity was disarming ...

SERGE.   What about me?

MARC.   What about you?

SERGE.   Do you have any idea what binds you to me? ...

MARC.   That's a question that could take us down a very long road ...

SERGE.   Lead on. *(Short silence.)*

MARC.   ... I'm sorry I upset Yvan.

SERGE.   Ah! At last you've said something approximately human ... What makes it worse is that the motel painting he has hanging on his wall was, I'm afraid, painted by his father.

MARC.   It was? Shit.

SERGE.   Yes ...

MARC.   But you said ...

SERGE.   Yes, yes, but I remembered as soon as I'd said it.

MARC.   Oh, shit ...

SERGE.   Mm ... *(Slight pause. The doorbell rings. Serge goes to answer it. Yvan enters immediately, talking as he arrives.)*

YVAN.   Yvan returns! The elevator was full, I plunged down the stairs, clattering all the way down thinking, a coward, an amoeba, no substance, I thought I'll come back with a gun and blow his head off, then he'll see how spineless and obsequious I am, I got to the lobby and I said to myself, listen, pal, you haven't been in therapy for six years to wind up shooting your best friend and you haven't been in therapy for six years without learning that some deep anxiety must lie behind his insane aggression, so I relaunch myself, telling myself as I mount the penitential stair, this is a cry for help, I have to help Marc, if it's the last thing I do ... In fact the other day I discussed you both with Finklezohn ...

SERGE.   You discussed us with Finklezohn?

YVAN.   I discuss everything with Finklezohn.

SERGE.   And why exactly were you discussing us?

MARC.   I forbid you to discuss me with that asshole.

YVAN.   You're in no position to forbid me anything.

SERGE.   Why were you discussing us?

YVAN.   I knew your relationship was under a strain and I wanted Finklezohn to explain ...

SERGE.   And what did the bastard say?

YVAN.   He said something kind of amusing ...

MARC.   They're allowed to give their opinions?

YVAN.   No, they never give their opinions, but this time he did give his opinion, he made a gesture and he never makes a gesture, he's always cold, I sometimes say to him, for God's sake, move around a little! ...

SERGE.   All right, what did he say?

MARC.   Who gives a fuck what he said?

SERGE.   What did he say?

MARC.   What possible interest could we have in what he said?

SERGE.   I want to know what the bastard said, all right? Shit! *(Yvan reaches into his jacket pocket.)*

YVAN.   You want to know? ... *(He fetches out a piece of folded paper.)*

MARC.   You took notes?

YVAN.   *(Unfolding it.)* I wrote it down because it was complicated ... Should I read it to you?

SERGE.   Go on.

YVAN.   ... "If I'm who I am because I'm who I am and you're who you are because you're who you are, then I'm who I am and you're who you are. If, on the other hand, I'm who I am because you're who you are and if you're who you are because I'm who I am, then I'm not who I am and you're not who you are ..." *(Short silence.)*

MARC.   How much do you pay this man?

YVAN.   Four hundred francs a session, twice a week.

MARC.   Great. You're very lucky, to be getting the benefit of this man's experience.

SERGE.   Absolutely! ... We'd really appreciate it if you'd make a copy for us.

MARC.   Yes, it's bound to come in handy. *(Yvan carefully refolds the piece of paper.)*

YVAN.   You're wrong. It's very profound.

MARC.   If it's because of him you've come back here to turn the other cheek, you should be grateful to him. He's cut off your balls, but you're happy, that's all that counts.

YVAN. *(To Serge.)* And all this because he doesn't want to believe I like your Antrios.

SERGE. I don't give a fuck what you think of it. Either of you.

YVAN. The more I see it, the more I like it, honest.

SERGE. Let's stop talking about the painting, shall we; once and for all. I have no interest in discussing if further.

MARC. Why are you so touchy?

SERGE. I am not touchy, Marc. You've told us what you think. Fine. The subject is closed.

MARC. You're getting upset.

SERGE. I am not getting upset. I'm exhausted.

MARC. See, if you're touchy about it, it means you're too caught up in other people's opinions ...

SERGE. I'm exhausted, Marc. This is completely pointless ... To tell you the truth, I'm really on the brink of getting bored with the both of you.

YVAN. Let's go eat.

SERGE. You go, why don't you go off together?

YVAN. No! It's so rare the three of us are together.

SERGE. Just as well, by the look of it.

YVAN. I don't understand what's going on. Can't we just calm down? There's no reason to insult each other, especially over a painting.

SERGE. You realize all this "calm down" and waving the white flag is just adding fuel to the fire! Is this a new thing?

YVAN. I will not be undermined.

MARC. Very impressive. Maybe I should go to this Finkel-zohn! ...

YVAN. You can't. There are no vacancies. What's that you're eating?

MARC. Gelsemium.

YVAN. I've given in to the logic of events, marriage, children, death. Stationery. What else can happen? *(Moved by a sudden impulse, Serge picks up the Antrios and takes it back where he found it, in the next room. He returns immediately.)*

MARC. We're not worthy to look at it ...

34

SERGE.   Exactly.

MARC.   Or are you afraid, if it stays in my presence, you'll wind up looking at it through my eyes? ...

SERGE.   No. You know what Paul Valery says? And I'd go quite a bit further.

MARC.   I don't give a fuck what Paul Valery says.

SERGE.   You've stopped liking Paul Valery?

MARC.   Don't quote Paul Valery at me.

SERGE.   But you used to love Paul Valery.

MARC.   I don't give a fuck what Paul Valery says.

SERGE.   But I discovered him through you. You're the one who got me into Paul Valery.

MARC.   Don't quote Paul Valery at me, I don't give a fuck what Paul Valery says.

SERGE.   What do you give a fuck about?

MARC.   I give a fuck about you buying that painting.

I give a fuck about you spending two hundred grand on that piece of shit.

YVAN.   Don't start again, Marc!

SERGE.   I'm going to tell you what I give a fuck about — since everyone is coming clean — I give a fuck about your snickering and insinuations, your suggestion that I also think this picture is a grotesque joke. You've refused to admit that I could feel a genuine attachment to it.

You've tried to set up some kind of loathsome complicity between us. And that's what's made me feel, Marc, to use your expression, how little binds us together these days, your perpetual display of distrust.

MARC.   It's true I can't imagine you genuinely loving that painting.

YVAN.   But why?

MARC.   Because I love Serge and I can't love the Serge who's capable of buying that painting.

SERGE.   Why do you say, buying, why don't you say, loving?

MARC.   Because I can't say loving, I can't believe loving.

SERGE.   So why would I buy it, if I didn't love it?

MARC.   That's the nub of the question.

SERGE.   *(To Yvan.)* See how smug he is! I'm trying to be

35

straightforward and he responds in this pompous heavy-handed tone. *(To Marc.)* And it never crossed your mind for a second, however improbable it might seem, that I might really love it and that your vicious, inflexible opinions and your vile assumption of complicity might be hurtful to me?

MARC.   No.

SERGE.   When you asked me what I thought of Paula — a girl who once spent an entire dinner party maintaining Elhers Danlos Syndrome could be cured homeopathically — did I say I found her ugly, repellent and totally charmless? I could have.

MARC.   Is that what you think of Paula?

SERGE.   What's your theory?

YVAN.   No, of course he doesn't think that! You couldn't possibly think that of Paula!

MARC.   Answer me.

SERGE.   You see the effect you can have!

MARC.   Do you think what you just said about Paula?

SERGE.   Worse, actually.

YVAN.   No!

MARC.   Worse, Serge? Worse than repellent? Will you explain how someone can be worse than repellent?

SERGE.   Interesting! When it's something that concerns you personally, I see words can bite a little deeper! ...

MARC.   Serge, will you explain how someone can be worse than repellent ...

SERGE.   No need to take that frosty tone. Perhaps it's — let me try and answer you — perhaps it's the way she waves away cigarette smoke.

MARC.   The way she waves away cigarette smoke ...

SERGE.   Yes. The way she waves away cigarette smoke.

What appears to you a gesture of no significance, what you think of as a harmless gesture is in fact the opposite, and the way she waves away cigarette smoke sits right at the heart of her repellentness.

MARC.   You're speaking to me of Paula, the woman who shares my life, in these intolerable terms, because you disapprove of her method of waving away cigarette smoke? ...

SERGE.   That's right. Her method of waving away cigarette

smoke condemns her out of hand.

MARC.   Serge, before I completely lose control, you'd better explain yourself.

   This is very serious, what you're doing.

SERGE.   A normal woman would say, I'm sorry, I find the smoke a bit uncomfortable, would you mind moving your ashtray, but not her, she doesn't deign to speak, she describes her contempt in the air with this calculated gesture, wearily malicious, this hand movement she imagines is imperceptible, the implication of which is to say, go on, smoke, smoke, it's pathetic but what's the point of calling attention to it, which means you can't tell if it's you or your cigarette that's getting up her nose.

YVAN.   You're exaggerating!

SERGE.   You notice he doesn't say I'm wrong, he says I'm exaggerating, but he doesn't say I'm wrong. Her method of waving away cigarette smoke reveals a cold, condescending and narrow-minded nature. Just what you're in the process of acquiring yourself. It's a shame, Marc, it's a real shame you've taken up with such a life-denying woman ...

YVAN.   Paula is not life-denying! ...

MARC.   Take back everything you've just said, Serge.

SERGE.   No.

YVAN.   Yes, you have to!

MARC.   Take back what you just said ...

YVAN.   Take it back, take it back! This is ridiculous!

MARC.   Serge, for the last time, I demand you take back what you've just said.

SERGE.   In my view, the two of you are an aberration. A pair of fossils. (*Marc throws himself at Serge. Yvan rushes forward to get between them.*)

MARC.   (*To Yvan.*) Get away! ...

SERGE.   (*To Yvan.*) Mind your own business! ... (*A kind of bizarre struggle ensues, very short, which ends with a blow mistakenly landing on Yvan.*)

YVAN.   Shit! ... shit! ...

SERGE.   Show me, show me ... (*Yvan is groaning. More than is necessary, it would seem.*) Come on, show me! ... That's all right ... It's nothing ... Wait a minute ... (*He goes out and comes back with a compress.*)

YVAN. ... You're complete freaks, both of you.

SERGE. Here you are, hold that on it for a while.

YVAN. Two normal men gone completely insane!

SERGE. Don't get excited.

YVAN. That really hurt! ... If I find out you've burst my eardrum! ...

SERGE. Of course not.

YVAN. How do you know? You're not ear, nose and throat! ... Two old friends, educated people ! ...

SERGE. Just calm down.

YVAN. You can't demolish somebody because you don't like her method of waving away cigarette smoke! ...

SERGE. Yes, you can.

YVAN. Well, all right, but it doesn't make any sense.

SERGE. What do you know about sense?

YVAN. That's right, attack me, keep attacking me! ... I could be hemorrhaging internally, I've just seen a mouse running by! ...

SERGE. It's a rat.

YVAN. A rat?

SERGE. He comes and goes.

YVAN. You have a rat?!

SERGE. Don't take the compress away, leave it where it is.

YVAN. What's the matter with you? ... What's happened between you?

   Something must have happened for you to get this demented.

SERGE. I've bought a work of art which makes Marc uncomfortable.

YVAN. You're starting again! ... You're in a downward spiral, both of you, you can't stop yourselves ... It's like me and Colette. The most pathological relationship you can imagine!

SERGE. Who's Colette?

YVAN. My step-mother!

SERGE. Oh, you haven't mentioned her for a while. *(Brief silence.)*

MARC. Why didn't you tell me right away what you thought about Paula?

SERGE. I didn't want to upset you.

MARC. No, no, no ...

SERGE. What do you mean, no, no, no? ...

MARC. No. When I asked you what you thought of Paula, what you said was: she's a perfect match for you.

SERGE. Yes ...

MARC. Which sounded positive, coming from you.

SERGE. Sure ...

MARC. Given the state you were in at the time.

SERGE. All right, what are you trying to prove?

MARC. But today, your assessment of Paula, or in other words me, is far harsher.

SERGE. ... I don't understand.

MARC. Of course you understand.

SERGE. I don't.

MARC. Since I can no longer support you in your frenzied, though recent, craving for novelty, I've become "condescending," "narrow-minded" ... "fossilised" ...

YVAN. I'm in agony! It's like something's drilling through my brain!

SERGE. Have a sip of brandy.

YVAN. What do you think? ... If something's shaken loose in my brain, don't you think alcohol's a little risky?

SERGE. Do you want an aspirin?

YVAN. Aspirin — Well, hm ...

SERGE. What the fuck do you want?

YVAN. Don't worry about me. Carry on with your preposterous conversation, don't pay any attention to me.

MARC. Easier said than done.

YVAN. You might squeeze out a drop of compassion. But no.

SERGE. I don't mind your spending time with Paula. I don't resent you being with Paula.

MARC. You have no reason to resent it.

SERGE. But you ... you resent me ... well, I was about to say, for being with the Antrios!

MARC. Yes!

SERGE. I'm missing something here.

MARC. I didn't replace you with Paula.

SERGE.   Are you saying, I replaced you with the Antrios?

MARC.   Yes,

SERGE.   ... I replaced you with the Antrios?

MARC.   Yes. With the Antrios ... and everything it implies.

SERGE.   *(To Yvan.)* Do you understand what he's talking about?

YVAN.   I couldn't care less, you're both insane.

MARC.   In my time, you'd never have bought that picture.

SERGE.   What's that supposed to mean, in your time?

MARC.   The time when you made a distinction between me and other people, when you judged things by my standards.

SERGE.   Was there such a time?

MARC.   That's just cruel ... And petty.

SERGE.   No, I assure you, I'm staggered.

MARC.   And if Yvan hadn't turned into such a sponge, he'd back me up.

YVAN.   Keep going, keep going, it's water off a duck's back.

MARC.   *(To Serge.)* There was a time you were proud to be my friend ... You congratulated yourself on my being a maverick, on my taste for standing apart. You enjoyed exhibiting me untamed to your circle, you, whose life was so normal. I was your alibi. But ... eventually, I suppose, that kind of affection dries up ... Belatedly, you claim your independence.

SERGE.   I like "Belatedly."

MARC.   But I detest your independence. Its violence. You've abandoned me. I've been betrayed. As far as I'm concerned, you're a traitor. *(Silence.)*

SERGE.   *(To Yvan.)* ... If I understand correctly, he was my mentor! ... *(Yvan doesn't respond. Marc stares at Serge contemptuously. Slight pause.)* And if I loved you as my mentor ... what was the nature of your feelings?

MARC.   You can guess.

SERGE.   Yes, yes, but I want to hear you say it.

MARC.   ... I loved the way you saw me. I was flattered. I was always grateful to you for thinking of me as a man apart. I even thought being a man apart was a somehow superior condition, until one day you pointed out to me that it wasn't.

SERGE.   This is very alarming.

MARC. It's the truth.

SERGE. What a disaster ... !

MARC. Yes, what a disaster!

SERGE. What a disaster!

MARC. Especially for me ... Whereas you've found a new family. Your penchant for idolatry has unearthed new objects of worship. The Artist! ... Deconstruction! *(Short silence.)*

YVAN. What is deconstruction? ...

MARC. You don't know about deconstruction? ... Ask Serge, he's very much on top of the subject ... *(To Serge.)* To convince me some ridiculous artwork is comprehensible, you pick a word from *Builders Weekly* ... Oh, you're smiling! You see, when you smile like that, I think there's still some hope, like an idiot ...

YVAN. Why don't you make up? And let's enjoy ourselves this evening. All this is ludicrous!

MARC. ... It's my fault. We haven't seen much of one another lately. I've been away and you started mixing with the high end ... the Robsons ... The Desprez-Couderts ... that dentist, Roger Hallier ... he's the one who ...

SERGE. No, no, no, no, not at all, he's from another world, he only likes conceptual art ...

MARC. It's all the same thing.

SERGE. No, it's not all the same thing.

MARC. You see, more evidence of how I let you slip away ... Now when we talk we can't even make ourselves understood.

SERGE. I had no idea whatsoever — really, it's come as a complete surprise — how much I was under your influence. The extent to which you owned me.

MARC. Or didn't own you, as it turns out ... You should never leave your friends unchaperoned. Your friends need to be chaperoned, otherwise they'll get away ... Look at poor Yvan, whose chaotic behavior used to delight us, we've allowed him to become this timid stationer ... Practically married ... He brought us his originality and now he's making every effort to piss it away.

SERGE. Us! He brought us! Do you know what you're saying? Everything has to revolve around you! Why can't you learn to love people for themselves, Marc?

MARC.   What does that mean, for themselves?

SERGE.   For what they are.

MARC.   But what are they?! What are they?! ... Apart from my faith in them? ... I'm desperate to find a friend who has some kind of prior existence. So far, I've had no luck. I've had to mold you ... But you see, it never works. There comes a day when your creature has dinner with the Desprez-Couderts and, to confirm his new status, goes off and buys a white painting. *(Silence.)*

SERGE.   So here we are at the end of a fifteen-year friend-ship ...

MARC.   Yes ...

YVAN.   Pathetic ...

MARC.   See, if only we'd managed to have a normal discussion, I mean, if only I'd been able to express myself without losing my temper ...

SERGE.   Well? ...

MARC.   Nothing ...

SERGE.   Yes. Go on. Why can't we exchange one single dispas-sionate word?

MARC.   I don't believe in the values that dominate contempo-rary Art. The rule of novelty. The rule of surprise. Surprise is dead meat, Serge. No sooner conceived than dead.

SERGE.   All right. So?

MARC.   That's all.

That's what my appeal to you was. My surprise value ...

SERGE.   What are you talking about?

MARC.   A surprise that's lasted quite a while, I'll admit.

YVAN.   Finklezohn is a genius.

I told you he understood the whole thing!

MARC.   I'd prefer it if you stopped umpiring, Yvan, and stop-ped imagining you're not fully implicated in this conversation.

YVAN.   You want to implicate me, I refuse. What does it have to do with me? I've already got a burst eardrum, you work things out for yourselves!

MARC.   See, Yvan, what I can't bear about you at the moment — quite apart from what I've already told you — is your craving to put Serge and me on the same level. You would like us to be equal. To indulge your cowardice. Talking on an equal footing, equal the way you thought of us when we were friends. But we were never equal, Yvan. You have to choose.

YVAN. I have chosen.

MARC. Excellent.

SERGE. I don't need a supporter.

MARC. You're not going to turn the poor boy down, are you?

YVAN. Why do we see each other, if we hate each other? It's obvious we do hate each other! I mean, I don't hate you, but you hate each other! And you hate me! So why do we see each other? ... I was looking forward to a relaxing evening after a ridiculously crazed week, meeting my two best friends, going to the movies, having a good time, getting away from all these dramas ...

SERGE. Are you aware that you've talked about nothing but yourself?

YVAN. Well, who are you talking about? Everybody talks about themselves!

SERGE. You fuck up our evening, you ...

YVAN. I fuck up your evening?! ...

SERGE. Yes.

YVAN. I fuck up your evening?! I?! I fuck up your evening?!

MARC. Yes, yes, don't get excited!

YVAN. You're saying it's me who fucked up your evening?! ...

SERGE. How many more times are you going to say it?

YVAN. Just answer the question, are you saying it's me who fucked up your evening?! ...

MARC. You arrive three-quarters of an hour late, you don't apologize, you swamp us with your domestic woes ...

SERGE. And your inertia, your sheer neutral spectator's inertia has lured Marc and me into the worst excesses.

YVAN. You, too! You're starting in on me, too?

SERGE. Yes, because on this subject I'm entirely in agreement with him. You create the conditions of conflict.

MARC. You've been piping up with this finicky, subservient voice of reason ever since you arrived, it's intolerable.

YVAN.   You know I could burst into tears ... I could start crying right now ... I'm very close to tears.

MARC.   Cry.

SERGE.   Cry.

YVAN.   Cry! You're telling me to cry!

MARC.   You've got every reason to cry, you're losing your two best friends, you're marrying a gorgon.

YVAN.   So is that it? It's all over!

MARC.   You said it yourself, what's the point of seeing each other, if we hate each other?

YVAN.   What about my wedding? You're my witnesses, remember?

SERGE.   Find someone else.

YVAN.   I can't!

MARC.   You can pick someone else at the last minute.

YVAN.   You're not allowed to!

SERGE.   Of course you are!

YVAN.   You're not! ...

MARC.   Don't panic, we'll come.

SERGE.   But what you should do is cancel the wedding.

MARC.   He's right.

YVAN.   Oh, shit! What have I ever done to you? Shit! *(He bursts into tears. Time passes.)*

This is savage, what you're doing! You could have had your fight after the 12ᵗʰ, but no, you're determined to ruin my wedding, a wedding which is already a catastrophe, which has made me lose ten pounds and now you're totally fucking it up! The only two people whose presence guaranteed some spark of satisfaction are determined to destroy one another, just my luck! ... *(To Marc.)* You think I like packs of Filofax paper or rolls of Scotch tape, you think any normal man wakes up one day desperate to sell expandable document wallets? ... What am I supposed to do? I farted around for forty years, I made you laugh, oh, yes, wonderful, I made all my friends laugh their heads off playing the fool, but at night, who was left solitary as a rat? Who crawled back into his hole every night all on his own? This buffoon, dying of loneliness, who'd switch on anything that talks and who does he find on the answering machine? His mother.

His mother. And his mother. *(A short silence.)*

MARC.   Don't get so upset.

YVAN.   Don't get so upset! Who upset me in the first place? Look at me. I don't have your refined sensibilities. I'm not a heavyweight. I don't have an opinion.

MARC.   Calm down ...

YVAN.   Don't tell me to calm down! What possible reason do I have to calm down, are you trying to drive me crazy, telling me to calm down? Calm down's the worst thing you can say to someone who's lost his calm. I'm not like you, I don't want to be an authority figure, I don't want to be a point of reference, I don't want to be self sufficient, I just want to be your friend Yvan the joker! Yvan the joker! *(Silence.)*

SERGE.   Could we try to steer clear of pathos? ...

YVAN.   I'm finished. You got anything to nibble on? Anything, just to keep from passing out.

SERGE.   I've got some olives.

YVAN.   Hand them over. *(Serge reaches for a little bowl of olives and hands it to him.)*

SERGE.   *(To Marc.)* Want some? *(Marc nods. Yvan hands him the bowl. They eat olives.)*

YVAN.   Is there somewhere to put the ...

SERGE.   Yes. *(He fetches a saucer and puts it on the table. Pause.)*

YVAN.   *(Still eating olives)* ... To think we've reached these extremes ... Apocalypse because of a white square.

SERGE.   It's not white.

YVAN.   A piece of white shit! ... *(He's seized by uncontrollable laughter.)* That's what it is, a piece of white shit! ... Face it, pal ... You buying this thing is demented ...*(Marc laughs, caught up in Yvan's extravagance. Serge leaves the room. He returns immediately with the Antrios.)*

SERGE.   Do you have one of your famous felt-tips? ...

YVAN.   What for? ... You're not going to draw on the painting.

SERGE.   Do you or don't you?

YVAN.   Just a minute ... *(He goes through the pockets of his jacket.)* Yes ... A blue one ...

SERGE.   Give it to me. *(Yvan hands the felt-tip to Serge. Serge takes the felt-tip, pulls the top off it, examines the tip for a moment, puts the top back on. He looks up at Marc and throws him the felt-tip. Marc catches it. Slight pause. To Marc.)* Go on! *(Silence.)* Go on! *(Marc approaches the painting ... He looks at Serge ... Then he takes the top off the felt-tip.)*

YVAN.   You're not going to do it! ... *(Marc is looking at Serge.)*

SERGE.   Come on.

YVAN.   You're raving lunatics, both of you! *(Marc leans toward the painting. Under Yvan's horrified gaze, he draws the felt-tip along one of the diagonal streaks. Serge remains impassive. Then, carefully, on the slope, Marc draws a little skier with a woolly hat. When he's finished, he straightens up and contemplates his work. Serge remains adamantine. Yvan is as if turned to stone. Silence. Marc tries a smile. He puts the top back on and playfully throws the pen to Yvan, who catches it.)*

SERGE.   Well, I'm starving. You want to go eat?

* * *

(At Serge's. At the back, hanging on the wall, the Antrios. Standing in front of the canvas, Marc is holding a basin of water, into which Serge is dipping a little piece of cloth. Marc has rolled up his sleeves and Serge is wearing a little builder's apron which is too short for him. Round about are various cleaning products, bottles of white spirit and stain remover, rags and sponges. Moving very delicately, Serge puts the finishing touch to the cleaning of the painting. The Antrios is as white as ever. Marc puts down the basin and looks at the painting. Serge turns to Yvan, who's sitting off to one side. Yvan nods approvingly. Serge steps back and contemplates the picture in his turn. Silence.)

YVAN.   *(As if alone, speaking in a slightly muffled voice)* ... The day after the wedding, Catherine put her wedding bouquet and a little bag of sugared almonds on her mother's grave at the Mont-parnasse cemetery. I slipped away to cry behind a monument and in the evening, thinking again about this touching tribute, I started silently sobbing in my bed. I absolutely have to speak to Finklezohn about this tendency to cry, I cry all the time, it's not normal for someone my age. It started, or at least clearly revealed itself at Serge's, the evening of the white painting. After

Serge, in an act of pure madness, had demonstrated to Marc that he cared more about him than he did about his painting, we went and had dinner, chez Emile. Over dinner, Serge and Marc made the decision to try to reconstruct a relationship destroyed by word and deed.

At one point, one of them used the expression "trial period" and I burst into tears.

This expression, "trial period" applied to our friendship, set off in me an uncontrollable and ridiculous convulsion.

In fact, I can no longer stand any kind of rational argument, nothing formative in this world, nothing great or beautiful in this world has ever been born of rational argument. *(Pause. Serge dries his hands. He goes to empty the basin of water then puts away all the cleaning products, until there's no sign left of domestic activity. Once again, he looks at his painting. Then he turns and advances toward the audience.)*

SERGE.   When Marc and I succeeded in obliterating the skier, with the aid of Swiss soap plus added ox gall, recommended by Paula, I looked at the Antrios and turned to Marc:

"Did you know ink from felt-tips was washable?"

"No" Marc said ... "No, did you?"

"No" I said, very quickly, lying. I came within an inch of saying, yes I guess I did know. But how could I have launched our trial period with such a disappointing admission? ... On the other hand, was it right to start with a lie? ... A lie! Let's be reasonable. Why am I being so absurdly virtuous? Why does my relationship with Marc have to be so complicated? ... *(Gradually, the light begins to narrow down on the Antrios. Marc approaches the painting.)*

MARC.   Under the white clouds, snow is falling.

You can't see the white clouds, or the snow.

Or the cold, or the white glow of the earth.

A solitary man glides downhill on his skis.

The snow is falling.

It falls until the man disappears back into the landscape.

My friend Serge, who's one of my oldest friends, has bought a painting.

It's a canvas about five feet by four.
It represents a man who moves across a space
then disappears.

PROPERTY LIST

Cleaning products
White painting (SERGE)
Book, *De Vita Beata* by Seneca
Folded piece of paper (YVAN)
Compress (SERGE)
Bowl of olives (SERGE)
Saucer (SERGE)
Blue felt-tip pen (YVAN)
Basin of water (MARC)
Piece of cloth (SERGE)
Apron (SERGE)

SOUND EFFECTS

Doorbell

NEW PLAYS

★ **MOTHERS AND SONS by Terrence McNally.** At turns funny and powerful, MOTHERS AND SONS portrays a woman who pays an unexpected visit to the New York apartment of her late son's partner, who is now married to another man and has a young son. Challenged to face how society has changed around her, generations collide as she revisits the past and begins to see the life her son might have led. "A resonant elegy for a ravaged generation." –NY Times. "A moving reflection on a changed America." –Chicago Tribune. [2M, 1W, 1 boy] ISBN: 978-0-8222-3183-7

★ **THE HEIR APPARENT by David Ives, adapted from Le Légataire Universel by Jean-François Regnard.** Paris, 1708. Eraste, a worthy though penniless young man, is in love with the fair Isabelle, but her forbidding mother, Madame Argante, will only let the two marry if Eraste can show he will inherit the estate of his rich but miserly Uncle Geronte. Unfortunately, old Geronte has also fallen for the fair Isabelle, and plans to marry her this very day and leave her everything in his will—separating the two young lovers forever. Eraste's wily servant Crispin jumps in, getting a couple of meddling relatives disinherited by impersonating them (one, a brash American, the other a French female country cousin)—only to have the old man kick off before his will is made! In a brilliant stroke, Crispin then impersonates the old man, dictating a will favorable to his master (and Crispin himself, of course)—only to find that rich Uncle Geronte isn't dead at all and is more than ever ready to marry Isabelle! The multiple strands of the plot are unraveled to great comic effect in the streaming rhyming couplets of French classical comedy, and everyone lives happily, and richly, ever after. [4M, 3W] ISBN: 978-0-8222-2808-0

★ **HANDLE WITH CARE by Jason Odell Williams.** Circumstances both hilarious and tragic bring together a young Israeli woman, who has little command of English, and a young American man, who has little command of romance. Is their inevitable love an accident…or is it destiny, generations in the making? "A hilarious and heartwarming romantic comedy." –NY Times. "Hilariously funny! Utterly charming, fearlessly adorable and a tiny bit magical." –Naples News. [2M, 2W] ISBN: 978-0-8222-3138-7

★ **LAST GAS by John Cariani.** Nat Paradis is a Red Sox-loving part-time dad who manages Paradis' Last Convenient Store, the last convenient place to get gas—or anything—before the Canadian border to the north and the North Maine Woods to the west. When an old flame returns to town, Nat gets a chance to rekindle a romance he gave up on years ago. But sparks fly as he's forced to choose between new love and old. "Peppered with poignant characters [and] sharp writing." –Portland Phoenix. "Very funny and surprisingly thought-provoking." –Portland Press Herald. [4M, 3W] ISBN: 978-0-8222-3232-2

DRAMATISTS PLAY SERVICE, INC.
440 Park Avenue South, New York, NY 10016 212-683-8960 Fax 212-213-1539
postmaster@dramatists.com www.dramatists.com

NEW PLAYS

★ **ACT ONE by James Lapine.** Growing up in an impoverished Bronx family and forced to drop out of school at age thirteen, Moss Hart dreamed of joining the glamorous world of the theater. Hart's famous memoir *Act One* plots his unlikely collaboration with the legendary playwright George S. Kaufman and his arrival on Broadway. Tony Award-winning writer and director James Lapine has adapted Act One for the stage, creating a funny, heartbreaking and suspenseful celebration of a playwright and his work. "…brims contagiously with the ineffable, irrational and irrefutable passion for that endangered religion called the Theater." –NY Times. "…wrought with abundant skill and empathy." –Time Out. [8M, 4W] ISBN: 978-0-8222-3217-9

★ **THE VEIL by Conor McPherson.** May 1822, rural Ireland. The defrocked Reverend Berkeley arrives at the crumbling former glory of Mount Prospect House to accompany a young woman to England. Seventeen-year-old Hannah is to be married off to a marquis in order to resolve the debts of her mother's estate. However, compelled by the strange voices that haunt his beautiful young charge and a fascination with the psychic current that pervades the house, Berkeley proposes a séance, the consequences of which are catastrophic. "…an effective mixture of dark comedy and suspense." –Telegraph (London). "A cracking fireside tale of haunting and decay." –Times (London). [3M, 5W] ISBN: 978-0-8222-3313-8

★ **AN OCTOROON by Branden Jacobs-Jenkins. Winner of the 2014 OBIE Award for Best New American Play.** Judge Peyton is dead and his plantation Terrebonne is in financial ruins. Peyton's handsome nephew George arrives as heir apparent and quickly falls in love with Zoe, a beautiful octoroon. But the evil overseer M'Closky has other plans—for both Terrebonne and Zoe. In 1859, a famous Irishman wrote this play about slavery in America. Now an American tries to write his own. "AN OCTOROON invites us to laugh loudly and easily at how naïve the old stereotypes now seem, until nothing seems funny at all." –NY Times [10M, 5W] ISBN: 978-0-8222-3226-1

★ **IVANOV translated and adapted by Curt Columbus.** In this fascinating early work by Anton Chekhov, we see the union of humor and pathos that would become his trademark. A restless man, Nicholai Ivanov struggles to dig himself out of debt and out of provincial boredom. When the local doctor, Lvov, informs Ivanov that his wife Anna is dying and accuses him of worsening her condition with his foul moods, Ivanov is sent into a downward spiral of depression and ennui. He soon finds himself drawn to a beautiful young woman, Sasha, full of hope and energy. Finding himself stuck between a romantic young mistress and his ailing wife, Ivanov falls deeper into crisis, heading toward inevitable tragedy. [8M, 8W] ISBN: 978-0-8222-3155-4

DRAMATISTS PLAY SERVICE, INC.
440 Park Avenue South, New York, NY 10016 212-683-8960 Fax 212-213-1539
postmaster@dramatists.com www.dramatists.com

NEW PLAYS

★ **I'LL EAT YOU LAST: A CHAT WITH SUE MENGERS by John Logan.** For more than 20 years, Sue Mengers' clients were the biggest names in show business: Barbra Streisand, Faye Dunaway, Burt Reynolds, Ali MacGraw, Gene Hackman, Cher, Candice Bergen, Ryan O'Neal, Nick Nolte, Mike Nichols, Gore Vidal, Bob Fosse…If her clients were the talk of the town, she was the town, and her dinner parties were the envy of Hollywood. Now, you're invited into her glamorous Beverly Hills home for an evening of dish, dirty secrets and all the inside showbiz details only Sue can tell you. "A delectable soufflé of a solo show…thanks to the buoyant, witty writing of Mr. Logan" –NY Times. "80 irresistible minutes of primo tinseltown dish from a certified master chef." –Hollywood Reporter. [1W] ISBN: 978-0-8222-3079-3

★ **PUNK ROCK by Simon Stephens.** In a private school outside of Manchester, England, a group of highly-articulate seventeen-year-olds flirt and posture their way through the day while preparing for their A-Level mock exams. With hormones raging and minimal adult supervision, the students must prepare for their future — and survive the savagery of high school. Inspired by playwright Simon Stephens' own experiences as a teacher, PUNK ROCK is an honest and unnerving chronicle of contemporary adolescence. "[A] tender, ferocious and frightning play." –NY Times. "[A] muscular little play that starts out funny and ferocious then reveals its compassion by degrees." –Hollywood Reporter. [5M, 3W] ISBN: 978-0-8222-3288-9

★ **THE COUNTRY HOUSE by Donald Margulies.** A brood of famous and longing-to-be-famous creative artists have gathered at their summer home during the Williamstown Theatre Festival. When the weekend takes an unexpected turn, everyone is forced to improvise, inciting a series of simmering jealousies, romantic outbursts, and passionate soul-searching. Both witty and compelling, THE COUNTRY HOUSE provides a piercing look at a family of performers coming to terms with the roles they play in each other's lives. "A valentine to the artists of the stage." –NY Times. "Remarkably candid and funny." –Variety. [3M, 3W] ISBN: 978-0-8222-3274-2

★ **OUR LADY OF KIBEHO by Katori Hall.** Based on real events, OUR LADY OF KIBEHO is an exploration of faith, doubt, and the power and consequences of both. In 1981, a village girl in Rwanda claims to see the Virgin Mary. Ostracized by her schoolmates and labeled disturbed, everyone refuses to believe, until impossible happenings appear again and again. Skepticism gives way to fear, and then to belief, causing upheaval in the school community and beyond. "Transfixing." –NY Times. "Hall's passionate play renews belief in what theater can do." –Time Out [7M, 8W, 1 boy] ISBN: 978-0-8222-3301-5

DRAMATISTS PLAY SERVICE, INC.
440 Park Avenue South, New York, NY 10016 212-683-8960 Fax 212-213-1539
postmaster@dramatists.com www.dramatists.com

NEW PLAYS

★ **AGES OF THE MOON by Sam Shepard.** Byron and Ames are old friends, reunited by mutual desperation. Over bourbon on ice, they sit, reflect and bicker until fifty years of love, friendship and rivalry are put to the test at the barrel of a gun. "A poignant and honest continuation of themes that have always been present in the work of one of this country's most important dramatists, here reconsidered in the light and shadow of time passed." –NY Times. "Finely wrought...as enjoyable and enlightening as a night spent stargazing." –Talkin' Broadway. [2M] ISBN: 978-0-8222-2462-4

★ **ALL THE WAY by Robert Schenkkan. Winner of the 2014 Tony Award for Best Play.** November, 1963. An assassin's bullet catapults Lyndon Baines Johnson into the presidency. A Shakespearean figure of towering ambition and appetite, this charismatic, conflicted Texan hurls himself into the passage of the Civil Rights Act—a tinderbox issue emblematic of a divided America—even as he campaigns for re-election in his own right, and the recognition he so desperately wants. In Pulitzer Prize and Tony Award–winning Robert Schenkkan's vivid dramatization of LBJ's first year in office, means versus ends plays out on the precipice of modern America. ALL THE WAY is a searing, enthralling exploration of the morality of power. It's not personal, it's just politics. "...action-packed, thoroughly gripping... jaw-dropping political drama." –Variety. "A theatrical coup...nonstop action. The suspense of a first-class thriller." –NY1. [17M, 3W] ISBN: 978-0-8222-3181-3

★ **CHOIR BOY by Tarell Alvin McCraney.** The Charles R. Drew Prep School for Boys is dedicated to the creation of strong, ethical black men. Pharus wants nothing more than to take his rightful place as leader of the school's legendary gospel choir. Can he find his way inside the hallowed halls of this institution if he sings in his own key? "[An] affecting and honest portrait...of a gay youth tentatively beginning to find the courage to let the truth about himself become known." –NY Times. "In his stirring and stylishly told drama, Tarell Alvin McCraney cannily explores race and sexuality and the graces and gravity of history." –NY Daily News. [7M] ISBN: 978-0-8222-3116-5

★ **THE ELECTRIC BABY by Stefanie Zadravec.** When Helen causes a car accident that kills a young man, a group of fractured souls cross paths and connect around a mysterious dying baby who glows like the moon. Folk tales and folklore weave throughout this magical story of sad endings, strange beginnings and the unlikely people that get you from one place to the next. "The imperceptible magic that pervades human existence and the power of myth to assuage sorrow are invoked by the playwright as she entwines the lives of strangers in THE ELECTRIC BABY, a touching drama." –NY Times. "As dazzling as the dialogue is dreamful." –Pittsburgh City Paper. [3M, 3W] ISBN: 978-0-8222-3011-3

DRAMATISTS PLAY SERVICE, INC.
440 Park Avenue South, New York, NY 10016 212-683-8960 Fax 212-213-1539
postmaster@dramatists.com www.dramatists.com